Dog Treatments & Alternative Home Remedies

~~~

Anne Cambridge

Table of Contents

Introduction

When you accept a dog into your home you are also about to welcome a new member of your household, and with that comes the total commitment and responsibility that goes with owning a pet. They will need love, nurturing and attention.

These are my dogs Saphie and Barney who I will mention a few times in this book.

As with our own health and well being there are some very compelling reasons why you should consider using home remedies for your dog.

These are just a few of the benefits of having home remedies close at hand.

They are cost effective. Using home remedies can save you money because they are more inexpensive than having a prescription from your vet as well as paying for the initial vet consultation. Some of my day to day ones like parsley for the teeth, or bicarbonate of soda for a kidney infection will cost you pennies.

You will eliminate any side effects that some prescription drugs have, you will learn more about this throughout the book.

You will have peace of mind. When you are confident with using home remedies as soon as a problem occurs you will know that you have a solution on hand to deal with it, or at least you will know it is available from your local store.

A dog's immune system has amazing powers to promote self-healing, and if you give your dog a good well balanced diet full of all the necessary nutrients you will maintain a good healthy animal.

Throughout my years of being a pet owner, there was nothing more terrifying to me or my four legged friends than visiting the vet's office.

Home care, at times, is the best solution to eliminate this panic from them. Every visit to the vet causes stress which subsequently affects and weakens the immune system and makes for a longer recovery time. Vet visits were always somewhat traumatic for my Animals, especially because of the whimpering dogs they could hear behind closed office doors and not understanding or knowing what was going on. Using home remedies in your 's familiar surroundings with people they trust and love, can only be a positive.

Being an animal lover, I wanted to eliminate these visits any way I could, or at least cut the number down to a minimum. So, with that in mind, I decided to research home treatments that were readily available. That's when I uncovered so many effective remedies that have been passed down through the generations. I hope you enjoy reading what I have discovered and become as enlightened as myself.

What began as finding alternatives to share with my friends, developed into a collection of valuable information any pet lover can benefit from. I decided to collate and publish an e-book to reach a much wider audience, which is what I have done. My journey was fascinating. Some of the information may be familiar to you, but most will surprise you.

More and more people are deciding to take responsibility for their health and are opting to research the internet to look for alternatives for themselves. It makes good sense to try and treat our pet's the same way. After all, are they not part of our family?

I hope that you will have a good grasp of how to treat your pet naturally by the time you're done reading this book. Many of the remedies can be easily found in your home and are used on a daily basis by us all.

I first became aware of how alternative therapies can help to soothe many diseases and ailments when I worked as a trained nurse in two Hospices. The medical team works side-by-side with conventional medicine, as the doctors and staff are encouraged to use whatever resources they can to make a patient more comfortable. My transition from helping dogs to Animals comes as no surprise to people who know me.

If your dog is currently undergoing treatment, it may be a good idea to share any thoughts and ideas you might have with your veterinary professional.

The recommendations in this book can only enhance and support any ongoing treatments. These remedies may only take you so far in your dog's level of care and wellness, so it may be necessary to consult a professional for advice in creating an individualized care package.

I am not advocating that we never visit the vet again, far from it. There may come a time when your pet may require essential surgery, and I will continue to visit my vet if there are no other choices. But many times, as I explain, we can treat our pet with home remedies, especially after surgery.

Guide to Alternative Therapies

Complementary and alternative therapies

The above phrases have been branded many times by the media when illness or disease is discussed, and the conception is that they mean the same thing because they are always combined into one phrase. This is not the case.

Complementary therapy can be used alongside traditional and conventional medicine, and be part of that person's, or in our case, that pet's treatment. It can help with the emotional aspects of being able to endure pain, and will make you or your pet feel better.

Always check with your vet before starting any therapies

Alternative Therapy is something different as this is used instead of any conventional treatments that may have been recommended.

Both therapies and their respective practitioners believe in the body's ability to heal itself and, as such, use an understanding of the working of the body which does not tend to be studied by practitioners in conventional medicine. Recently, many more veterinarians have begun to believe that they can work side-by-side with alternative and complimentary practitioners.

Most treatments are non-invasive, and do not have the long term side effects that other medicines may have.

Acupuncture

There are acupuncture practitioners who specialize in animals and many of them have witnessed amazing results with pain control. This treatment involves inserting needles into specific areas of the animal and allowing the energy to flow. This is called chi. It is from an ancient Chinese practice and, in addition to pain control, it can cure chronic ailments.

Aromatherapy

The use of plant-based essential oils to treat all sorts of ailments–physical, emotional and mental–has been used by dogs for many years. Many veterinarians now believe the same results can be achieved with Animals.

For a quick fix, oils can be used in first aid. Arnica has a great history against bruising and in treating aches and pains. Calendula is a remarkable healing agent, suitable for scratches, cuts and raw skin, especially when the dog has had a tussle with another . This is not an aromatherapy fix, but if you see a bleeding cut or wound you can sprinkle cayenne pepper on it in an emergency. This enhances the clotting process and will help stop the bleeding. All of the above can be used easily, are widely available and are safe for use in treating dogs

Oils work in conjunction with the emotional and physical part of the dog, and takes into consideration that you are not just treating the main specific symptom. They have a positive effect on the animal's whole being–mind, body and spirit–and will not leave any undue toxic residue that many conventional and synthetic medicines do.

Essential oils

Geranium

Also known as aromatic essences, essential oils are extracted from a wide variety of trees. You may have heard of many of these, such as geranium, pine, eucalyptus, jasmine and, the most common, lavender. The oils are found within small glands inside the plants and have potent therapeutic properties. Many people describe them as "the soul" of the plant, which would also make it spiritual.

Lavender

How they work remains a mystery to us, but what we do know is that they have an active medicinal property, working like the flower essences influencing the positive energy force of an animal. The energy of the animal interacts with the energy of the oils to produce a healing effect.

If an animal's vital force becomes weakened, inevitably disease and illness will follow. Knowing your pet as well as you do, you will have noticed outward signs something is wrong. The root cause of the illness could be emotional and essentials oils will balance the vital force which brings your pet back into harmony and health.

How to use essential oils

Oils can used in a variety of ways, the most common being massage, which many dogs love. Oil inhalation is not as easy, but is still beneficial.

To combat fleas, which will be explained later on, you can bathe your pet in essential oils. This will soothe and heal many skin problems.

I have personally used a compress on my dog for muscle pain after she fell off a chair. Because she is a small breed, to her it was a great height. She loved the compress and allowed me to keep on for the entire hour. I think she liked the cuddling as well.

Inhalation

Inhalation is used to treat a dog that may have respiratory problems. It also works as a great disinfectant in small areas where your pet is living.

A diffuser has an electrical motor which allows a fine spray of essential oils to be pumped into the surrounding air. You can also use a burner which heats the oil by a candle or a burner ring with a warm light bulb.

Store your oils safely and correctly. Make sure they are not in direct sunlight and, because they are sensitive to heat, keep them at room temperature. They are best stored in tinted glass bottles and, if these particular protocols are followed, they should last a few years.

Dosage

Essential oils are very potent and should always be diluted if they are to be used directly on the skin, or if they are to be given internally. Use two teaspoons of base oil, i.e.: vegetable or almond oil and then add two to three drops of essential oil. You can use up to three different types of essential oils together.

Almond oil

Homeopathy

Homeopathy is an energy medicine, just like acupuncture and flower essences, and has a positive effect on the animal's vital force. The remedies activate the body's own healing mechanism according to a principle known as "like cures like". Translated, this means that conventional medicine will treat a specific illness with an antidote and homoeopathy will treat with a similar substance, only one that is much more potent.

Holistic treatment cares for each animal as an individual and allows them to heal from the inside out. Homoeopathic remedies stimulate the body's own healing mechanism but, by doing so, can aggravate or cause a pre-existing condition to flare up. Rashes can be more severe, digestive problems can worsen and the animal can develop a bout of diarrhoea.

This is actually a good sign the remedy is working because the animal's natural forces of recovery are in action. However, they are quick to pass so do not be too alarmed.

The remedies are taken from animal, plant and mineral sources, and are made by a qualified pharmacist. If you have researched thoroughly and successfully found a competent homoeopath, your animal will be in safe hands.

Homoeopathic remedies are diluted and leave virtually no trace or evidence of the original substance. This is the reason they are non-toxic.

Conventional medicines only suppress the symptoms and lower the status of the body by driving the disease deeper. Homoeopathy will not do this. With a correctly prescribed dose, it will safely and gently and, most importantly, permanently elevate the health of the body.

Dosage

The amount given to a dog is the same as that for humans as the size is not an important factor in determining how much to give. The frequency of the dose is important, depending on whether you are treating an acute or chronic disease.

Acute

For the first three hours give one tab every fifteen to twenty minutes. After the initial hour passes, give one tablet every hour for the rest of the day. Then give one tablet three times a day, for an additional few days until all the symptoms have disappeared.

If an illness is severe and you are not noticing any signs of improvement after a couple of hours, then it would be best to visit your vet. Observe your pet's reaction to the remedy, as any change occurring is a sign that healing is taking place. Very often, a good sign is that they are relaxed and will go to sleep.

Chronic

For one week, give one tablet three times a day, and then give one tablet twice a day for the following few weeks. Concerning long term conditions, one tablet per week for several weeks is normally sufficient.

If you find your pet is having an adverse reaction to the remedy, then stop immediately for twenty-four hours. Once the effects have subsided, you may recommence treatment. If the reaction occurs again, then use coffee or a strong **peppermint** as an antidote. There is a fine line between distinguishing if the animal is having a reaction, or if it is actually the correct remedy working as it should.

If you are uncertain, always seek a professional for advice.

Peppermint

How to give remedies

Do not touch the remedies. They must always be placed directly into the dogs mouth from either the container lid or a spoon. Always administer a remedy half an hour before or after a meal. If more than one remedy is to be given, always wait at least five minutes between doses.

For difficult dogs that don't like taking tablets, I find if you crush them and then add them to a small amount of milk, ice cream or, in my case, my dogs like **yoghurt**, it is much easier to dispense.

Unlike other alternative therapies, Homoeopathy will not work side by side with conventional medicine.

Bach Flower Essences were developed by a man called Edward Bach. He discovered in the 1930s that we are surrounded by many non-poisonous bushes, wild plants and trees in our English countryside that exerted genuine therapeutic effects on our emotional state which, in turn, was able to promote a physical balance in our body.

He truly believed that by correcting any emotional problems in our bodies, it would balance out and heal any physical dysfunction.

Dr Bach also believed that the mind showed the cause and onset of any disease much quicker than the body. Being a sensitive spiritual man, he believed that individual plants responded to the natural vibrations of certain mental states. His great insight and intuition led to discovering twelve plants which affected pathological mental states. He went on to develop and identify a total of thirty-eight individual flower essences. The most widely and well known one used today is the five-flower combination that we know as **Rescue Remedy.**

It escalated from then to a whole new breed of products being labelled as "Flower Essences". They originate from the same concept and principle, and are prepared from minerals, gems, and other matter. Veterinarians

21

have been using and prescribing these essences for many years because they believe they are beneficial in helping to heal the emotional and physical ills of Animals.

Although clinical tests have been inconclusive in explaining exactly how they work, essences have been particularly valuable in behavioural problems in dogs, with many positive results being seen.

Bach flower essences work by flooding the animal with a positive quality essence of a particular flower, thus correcting a negative emotional state. You would use **Rock Rose** for your pet if they have deep fears, panic or, for instance, during a thunderstorm or on fireworks night. The younger of my two dogs was terrified at first of fireworks until I gave him Rock Rose. He still doesn't like them, but does not experience the terror he had before.

Rock rose

Flower remedies do not treat a specific behaviour. They concentrate on a subtle emotional level and aim to create an emotional state that is calm, peaceful and happy. Essences are safe to use and non-toxic.

Whichever treatment you choose for your pet's wellness, if they are recuperating from an illness, it's important that you create a healing environment. They may have a special place or area that they feel comfortable, safe and cozy. Make sure it is draft-free and warm. Using plenty of soft bedding will prevent bed sores. A tip I came across recently was to use egg boxes squashed up and placed in a pillow case with some soft bedding on top. Always keep their water and food bowls nearby.

Your pet will not feel like playing, so be sure to educate your children on why they should not pester them while they are in the recovery stage. Normally, rice and chicken is advised in this stage, but they don't always want to eat. Make sure they are hydrated. An important thing to remember is they may be unable to get outside to relieve themselves, so please do not scold them for soiling indoors as this will only distress them further.

If you follow these simple tips with love and care, your pet will make a full recovery very quickly.

Storage of Essences

Because flower essences are liquid energy and can easily be influenced by other energies, it is very important that they are not stored anywhere near electrical equipment, like computers or televisions, and avoid direct sunlight. Like most conventional medicines, if the protocol is followed, flower essences can survive for at least five years.

Dosage

Again, the dosage for a dog is the same as with humans, usually three to four drops is added to their food or water. Be sure their drinking water is freshened every day. I have put the drops on my dogsnose and he has licked it off and seemed to like it. Alternatively by putting the drops directly onto the fur it will be absorbed into his system straight away.

Three to four times a day is the normal dosage to give for treatment, but in the case your pet is suffering from extreme stress and anxiety, you can administer every ten or twenty minutes until the anxiety has subsided.

There is no need to worry if other animals in your household have access to the food or water bowls. The dose will only be beneficial to the animal that actually needs it and are completely harmless to others.

Ageing

On average, and depending on the breed, dogs can live up to thirteen years. Smaller dogs tend to live longer and may live eighteen years or more.

Our care and attention to our Animals has changed because of expanding knowledge that only enhances their quality of living. Because of this they are able to reach their full potential and lead a happy and contented life.

But as our pets advance in age, the nature of disease changes. We are now seeing a wider range of age-related disorders and diseases that have been undiagnosed before. Metabolic diseases, general wear and tear, and other illnesses are resulting, such as heart disease and cancer. Senile dementia a disease normally associated with humans, and the early onset of Alzheimer's is now occurring in dogs.

There is a new field in veterinarian medicine which is being investigated and studied, as with people, and it's called geriatric medicine.

The aging process is similar to what we experience as humans. Loss of brain function starts for a dog by the time they reach between eleven and sixteen years of age, depending again of the breed. They may become disorientated, and the relationships they have with the family changes.

My dog is fourteen years old and now wants to sleep behind the sofa all day, only emerging for food or the occasional walk. About twenty percent of dogs over this age start to pass urine and faeces in the home without any warning.

Saphie behind the sofa

Many dogs also become confused with the home surroundings, sometimes bumping into furniture or taking longer to climb down a step to the back door. If your pet is female and spayed she will become more aggressive, whereas the male neutered dog becomes more passive.

Like people, as dogs get older they begin to experience the same changes we do like painful joints, decreased energy levels and weight gain.

We cannot alter this process in people any more than we can in dogs, but it's possible to help them in other ways. One method is to ensure they get enough exercise. If he is allowed to sleep all day without proper exercise his joints will become stiff and, subsequently trigger a decline in other organs.

You can actively slow the natural aging process by providing stimulation, mentally and physically. Your pet loves to be stroked and cuddled, so try mixing this with a gentle massage. This helps to loosen up any stiff joints and at the same time improves the circulation of blood to all parts of the body.

Multiple studies conducted in the 1980s showed that when the brain is stimulated with mental exercise, it grows in size. It does not produce more cells, but it is able to create new connections with other cells. By providing your dog with mental activities, you are able to slow down the natural decline of memory. So play some games that make him think!

Veterinarians have always been great advocates of diet and exercise and, together, they are extremely important to your pet's health. Practical ways to achieve a balance are twice daily walks. Even a short period will get the blood supply going which in turn will stop any stiffness setting into the joints.

I also believe it is mentally therapeutic that dogs go outside for exercise. My fourteen year old dog looks at me and, even though she can't say it, she is so happy to be out after I've encouraged her. They like nothing more than to socialise, sniff everything and chew grass. She is improving each day and now goes for longer walks which I believe is due in part to the **Salmon fish oil and Diatomaceous earth** I give her each morning with a plastic syringe.

I am lucky enough to live by the sea, and I sometimes look behind during our walk to see her just sitting and relaxing and staring out to sea.

I'm sure her mind is stimulated and also would like to think she is reminiscing of days past. So please be patient with your dog, you wouldn't drag your elderly parent along the road, would you? It'll be worth it in the end.

There is no need to play around with your dogs diet just because he is getting old. If he is happy and likes what he has been served all these years, there's no need to interfere with something that works just because you see a package that says Senior on it.

If your dog is becoming overweight, but it is not due to a lack of daily exercise, you will have to look at what you are feeding him.

As tempting as it is to feed your pet dog hand-outs from table leftovers, please resist. You are not doing your dog any good in the long term. A nice piece of ham is not something an older dog can handle and the food will be too rich for him to digest when he is older.

You may be encouraged by adverts to put your pet on a low-fat senior diet, but this can actually harm him. These diet foods are normally comprised of mostly grains, which are low in protein. It is in fact the opposite for older dogs as they benefit from protein because it aids in tissue repair. The only reason to avoid too much protein is if they have been diagnosed with a kidney problem or disease.

Supplements at least once a week, such as a good fish oil or fresh mackerel, are good for the older dog. Both of my dogs love these.

Try to find a supplement that has a good mix of antioxidants (Vitamins A C, and E) as well as selenium.

Salmon Fish Oil is one of the best daily supplements and has been proven to slow the progression of kidney disease. It also keeps the bowels of an older animal soft which is beneficial as they tend to get constipated when not getting enough exercise or being less mobile.

If your dog's appetite has decreased, and he has been checked over and been given a clean bill of health, it is likely because his sense of smell has diminished. You can try tantalizing his taste buds by adding smelly alternatives like tuna oil to his food.

Teeth maintenance in the older dog is very important because if they lose any of their teeth, they will not be able to eat properly. Do not allow any decay to go untreated as this will surely cause problems further down the line.

Advice and remedies for teeth and gum brushing are detailed in another chapter.

Chlorella

I came across this when researching how to get rid of mercury and metals in our systems, so I was aware of the benefits. I recently discovered it was also suitable for Animals and ageing.

When chlorella is added regularly to the diet, it markedly slows the ageing process and maintains youthful energy much longer. It helps normalize an animal's blood picture, improves liver and kidney function, and is a great detoxifier. Research has shown it improves the haemoglobin count, which boosts the delivery of oxygen to the system.

Chlorella is a single-celled freshwater algae packed with minerals, vitamins, amino acids and, most importantly, chlorophyll, which is one of nature's best cleansers and detoxifiers.

Dosage

You can give one gram of the powder to small dogs daily, mixed with food. I mix a cocktail and give in a plastic syringe because I like to know my dogs are getting the exact amount they should

Larger breeds can have up to three grams daily.

Vitamin E has been shown to slow down the oxidative damage aging has on tissues in older Animals and has also been shown to benefit circulation, the immune system and improve the dogs stamina and endurance.

Anaemia

If you notice your dog is not running around like he normally does, but is dragging around as if he has been to an all night rave, or is not too excited when it is suppertime, then he may be experiencing the first signs of anaemia.

I f you do suspect that your pet is anaemic take a look at his mouth checking the colour of the gums, they should be a healthy pink (although some dogs normally have black or brown mouths). If the inside of the mouth is quite pale then you should consult a vet, as it could also be a sign of an underlying problem.

Sometimes it is the medication that your pet has been digesting over a period of time ie: aspirin or anti inflammatory tablets that are actually causing bleeding in the digestive tract..In addition to this some drugs can attack healthy blood cells reducing the oxygen-carrying capacity of the blood.

1.For a quick fix for your pet give him foods that will boost the iron and B Vitamins he needs like Liver, which can be given daily over a period of one week.

2 .Kelp powder which contains iodine and other trace minerals.

3. Nutritional yeast along with B12 which can offer the same benefits as Liver.

4. Vitamin C give between 500 to 2,000 milligrams a day depending on the dog's size which will help with absorption of iron from the intestinal tract.

5. Green vegetables which contain iron and other minerals.

You can also give your dog **Blackstrap Molasses** which is a rich source of nutrients that provides vitamin B6, iron, calcium, copper, potassium, manganese and selenium. All of these vitamins and minerals are good for your pet and will offer several potential health benefits.

Blackstrap molasses is not as sweet as ordinary molasses so is easier for your pet to manage, and when used as a supplement is safe to take. As well as the vitamins and minerals present it also contains stigmastrol an ingredient that relieves arthritis and stiffness.

Supplements from a good health shop will aid the recovery and boost the production of red blood cells.

Try to keep your dog calm and relaxed as too much stress and exercise will increase the body's demand for oxygen, which is in short supply with a dog that has anaemia.

Anxiety

There is a strong emotional bond that ties a dog to its owner, and at times it can be extraordinarily intense. They watch anxiously when you leave the house, sleep on the floor by the bed or the couch, and follow you constantly from room to room around the house.

The love and depth of their dedication is so special to us, but it is also one of the reasons our dog's can become stressed and develop separation anxiety. This anxiety manifests itself to become extreme fear as soon as the owners leave the house. The way they cope with this is to continually bark–annoying to your next door neighbours, and by destroying furniture and other belongings.

This type of anxiety is often alleviated by wearing him out with a long walk before you leave the house. Exercise is a wonderful sedative and will normally knock them out for a good few hours.

You can also play a game called treasure hunt. Using some of his toys, stashed with treats, go out the door a couple of times playing with him while using your keys, so he associates this with the game and he understands you will be back.

If I am going to be gone from the house for a few hours I either put the TV on low, or play some calming music and it does seem to help.

Other types of anxiety can be nervous or even social if your pet becomes agitated around other dogs. Thunder and lightning storms and fireworks really cause stress for some dogs. Instead of my dog barney having to wear his earphones every fireworks night to drown out the sound of the fireworks as he is so frightened and nervous, he is now given four drops of rescue remedy before the celebrations start, and once during.

As you can see from the picture taken after, I would say it works!

Barney Chilling out

Many vets encourage you to try conventional drugs on an animal and usually this will be some type of anti-depressant, however they do have undesirable side effects.

Many pet owners are opting for alternatives. Rescue remedy has been used and trusted by dogs for many years and is now known to be as effective in dogs. It is one product from the whole range of **Bach Flower remedies** out there. Another flower option is Agrimony, which is given for hidden anxiety. This is beneficial when you know your pet will be distressed when you leave but they are hiding it, only for you to return and find they have been destructive.

Sweet Chestnut is for a dog that displays symptoms of deep despair when you leave them alone.

Sweet Chestnut

Red Chestnut is useful for the pet that is worried and anxious about being abandoned or neglected the minute the owner leaves the house or when left outside a shop and, even though they can see you, they still panic.

Red Chestnut

Put a few drops in their drinking water or, if you want to be sure they are getting enough, it is more effective to gently rub a few drops on his mouth and gums. In most cases this has immediate effect.

Dosage

These flower remedies can be given as often as three or four times a day. It is normally advisable to continue this schedule over an extended period of time.

Herbs

There are many calming herbs you can give and Chamomile is a favourite of mine. I use this often as a tea and it helps reduce the anxiety in stressed out dogs. It calms the nerves and induces sleep. You can give treats soaked in chamomile or make a tea and try to give him sips or, easier still, have small syringe handy and give it this way.

Chamomile

Lemon Balm is also effective in treating dogs prone to becoming excited and nervous.

Cooked oatmeal is nutritious as well as having a calming effect.

Valerian

This herb is well known and widely used by dogs and can be administered to dogs. It will reduce tension, excitability and anxiety.

Some nutritional supplements are specifically designed to treat anxiety and hyperactivity.

L-theanine

This is a non-protein amino acid found exclusively in tea plants, and is derived from green tea leaves. L-theanine has been found to directly stimulate the production of alpha brain waves, thus creating a state of deep relaxation. It has also been successfully used by dogs as a calming supplement.

Thiamine

Thiamine is a water-based soluble vitamin and is part of the B complex group. It has been shown to have an effect on the nervous system and can particularly calm and soothe anxious Animals. Sometimes, if there is a deficiency in your , this could be one of the main reasons they are anxious all the time.

Thiamine cannot be stored in the body. Any increased activity, such as stress or illness, can speed the metabolic rate and deplete normal levels.

When you purchase nutritional supplements from a reputable practitioner they will have guidelines and dosages for you to follow, so there's no need to feel concerned about proper administration.

Green tea contains a non-protein amino acid which helps dogs and animals relax. Be sure to give green tea at room temperature so as not to burn the 's mouth.

Essential oils such as Lavender have a great calming effect. You can add to a bandana for them to wear or roll it into a ball and place in the dogs sleeping area. Only mix about 5mls of the oil and try to dilute it, as lavender can be too overpowering for some dogs.

Homeopathic remedies will calm dogs with anxiety issues. The great thing about these is that the effect is almost instantaneous. If your pet suffers from anxiety caused by fireworks, thunder, or is nervous when travelling in the car, you can give one or more of the following remedies before an event you know will stress them.

Borax

Borax crystals

Dogs that are easily startled by sudden noises like fireworks or gunshots, if you happen to live in the country, will benefit from Borax. Other good candidates for Borax are dogs who may have a problem when going down stairs or who panic when you put them on the floor. This is because they have a fear of downward motion.

Passiflora incarnata

This has calming properties, but is not a sedative. It is good for Animals that are travelling or to calm a frightened animal.

Phosphorous

Dogs that benefit from this remedy can be normally sweet, mild-natured and gentle, but when they feel frightened or threatened in a stressful situation like a visit to the vet's, they can become explosive. They can also have a fear of thunder lightening and other extreme loud noises.

Rhododendron

Rhododendron has a positive effect on dogs that sense a storm is on the way. They are sensitive to this fact and their symptoms usually worsen just before the onset of bad weather.

The dosages of the homeopathic remedies above should be prescribed by a qualified practitioner.

Arthritis

Dogs, like people, will show signs that they are getting older and stiff and creaky joints come with age. Normally, larger dogs are more prone to develop arthritis than smaller varieties as they have to carry extra weight.

Arthritis is a painful condition that occurs when cartilage in a joint starts to break down for multiple reasons, including age and the onset of disease.

Painful joints

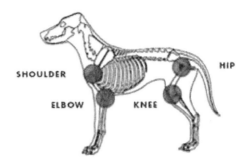

SHOULDER HIP ELBOW KNEE

If painful joints are present in an older pet, it is usually a sure indication that they are developing the early signs of arthritis.

They struggle to get up in the morning because being in the same position for a long period of time make the joints stiff. When they eventually do try to move, it will be painful and will take them much longer to get going.

Whatever the breed or age of your dog, a diagnosis of arthritis can and will cause them much pain and be very debilitating. The highest percentage of dogs suffering and developing arthritis tend to be those ten years of age or older.

Signs to look for in Arthritis

- Difficulty in walking

- Weight gain

- Mood or behaviour changes

- Movements that suggest joints are stiff or sore

- Sleeping a lot more

• Not as alert

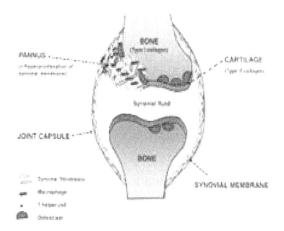

With the above guidelines, a pet owner will be able to spot the early signs of arthritis and hopefully begin to treat the pet at home.

I believe one of the very first signs you will notice is a dog that may be reluctant to walk as much, mainly because they are in pain. If they become irritable when handled and snappy when you try to pick them up, then painful joints may be the cause. I recently discovered that my older dog had arthritis purely by chance when she went in for a routine teeth clean.

On returning home she was in such severe pain and not from the cleaning, but from the fact she had been in placed in a position on the table for so long. It had irritated the arthritis present in her neck and while she was crying out in pain, an x-ray later revealed how bad the arthritis was.

So, if your dog is snappy or wants to be left alone it could be because, like us, it's painful when they are touched or moved. Thankfully, she is now on Salmon Fish Oil and it is really helping her. She is still snappy at times, but I believe it is more due to her age and being very spoilt!

They may also try to lick or chew the affected area and this is a sure sign inflammation and pain is present in the joint.

Are they taking a lot longer to get up from a reclining position after being at rest? Watch out for signs of lameness especially when jumping down from a height. If you suspect anything is wrong or they are exhibiting any of the above signs, begin using some of the recommendations below.

If you would like a diagnosis from a vet before self-medicating, the first step is to ask for a routine x-ray. This will give you peace of mind that it is only arthritis. Keep in mind, subjecting your pet to an x-ray will often require your pet to be sedated.

Conventional medicines prescribed after a diagnosis can be risky. Even some vets admit toxicity levels long term and the side effects with chronic use are uncertain. Trying alternatives first to see if the symptoms improve may prove effective and safe.

Always check with your vet if you are worried about the contra-indications of any other medicine they are taking, before trying alternative or home remedies.

Diet can play an important part in your pet's rehabilitation and getting back to leading a healthy, pain-free life. If a pet has arthritis, their body finds it difficult to metabolise calcium. Many pet foods today are geared towards providing meat products, but are low in calcium. Therefore, we have to supplement the diet with grains, which are high in calcium. If your dog is overweight it will not help the recovery, so a good diet to reduce excess weight is a must.

As I mentioned before, I give Salmon Fish Oil to both my dogs daily. It contains a large amount of Omega 3 fatty acids, EPA, DHA, as well as Omega 6 fatty acids. This not only helps with the inflammation of joints, but has all the nutrients to give your pet a healthy skin and a shiny coat.

You need to find foods that contain EPA and DHA. If your pet is partial to tuna or salmon, which are high in both, they can have a treat a few times a week.

Fortunately, there has been research conducted by Kansas State University regarding arthritic conditions in dogs. They compared the effects of giving Omega 3 fatty acid supplements versus no supplements with dogs that had developed Osteoarthritis.

The trial consisted of thirty-eight dogs that were randomly given commercial food with or without 3.5percent of Omega 3 fatty acids as fish oil. They recorded which were given the food with fish oil and they were evaluated throughout a ninety day trial. The dogs that consumed Omega 3 showed a significant improvement in areas such as lameness and weight bearing, when compared with dogs that were given food without the oil.

There has been good research proving that what humans are prescribed for joints, dogs can also take the main one being a mixture of Glucosamine and Chondroitin. These two combined, help to lubricate the joints, allowing more movement while stopping the scraping and rubbing that ultimately leads to scar tissue which develops into spurs and arthritis deterioration.

Glucosamine has an anti-inflammatory effect and improves the joint function. It also gives cartilage its strength structure and shock absorbing qualities. It is responsible for the formation of skin, bones, tendons and ligaments–all essential and found in high concentrations in the cartilage and connective tissue.

Chondroitin is essential for the resilience of the same cartilage and is also needed for the repair and formation of connective tissue. This combination can be easily absorbed by the animal and enables the body's own ability to manufacture collagen. This is most essential for the rebuilding of joints and allows synovial fluid to lubricate the joints. Collagen, known as the "glue that holds the body together", also gives tissues firmness and strength.

Vitamin C should be taken alongside as it is needed to stimulate the production of collagen. Vitamin C aids in the production and controls tissue growth, especially after injury. Arthritis is an injury, too, and is what has happened to the joints after they have become inflamed with age. Sometimes the dogs diet is partially to be blamed. Vitamin C has amazing healing properties and is good for the pet's immune system.

Vitamin C will help prevent further joint deterioration and keep the tissue healthy. The powder form is easy to sprinkle on your pet's food.

Whenever I have a painful joint, an ice pack over the area gives me relief. I know it sounds difficult to imagine, but if you have a pet that likes cuddles then they will tolerate an ice pack for just a short while.

Aspirin is an over-the-counter remedy that works well to relieve joint pain and inflammation. Be sure to check the dosage with a vet. It is cheaper to buy baby aspirin, but you need to calculate the dose ratio to your pet's weight. Aspirin is only for short term use, just to help at the onset of pain.

Devil's claw in tincture format acts quickly and moves directly into the bloodstream. This is good for the maintenance of healthy bones and joints, and allows for more suppleness and easier movement. The anti-inflammatory properties present reduce pain, swelling and stiffness in the joints and muscles.

Garlic taken as a supplement has antibiotic, antiseptic and antiviral characteristics, which target the symptoms of rheumatism, arthritis and any

inflammation affecting the joint.

Garlic

Celery seed has a wide range of uses. It has been known to support the natural reduction of excess uric acid in the joints–one of the main causes of pain and inflammation.

Rosehips are a rich source of Vitamin C and can help maintain and keep joints healthy. Widely known to be one of nature's richest sources of Vitamin C, it is well known to be a supporter of the immune system. It aids in the absorption of essential minerals, which are needed if we are to treat inflammation in the joints.

Rosehips can be used daily as a natural support for the joints and as a preventative option as well.

Coconut Oil

I have discovered coconut oil will help fight the pain associated with arthritis, with just a half of a teaspoon daily. I buy a jar and give my dogs a teaspoonful, too. They actually like it and lick it easily off the spoon.

Diatomaceous earth

One of my dog walking friends was preparing to take some time to spend with her fourteen year old dog , thinking he had come to the end of his life. He was lethargic and his appetite was poor. She decided to try giving him a half teaspoon of Diatomaceous earth daily, as the properties in the powder are supposed to give dogs more energy. . Now many of us are also taking it and my nails are growing. I have also discovered an increase in my energy levels. Diatomaceous earth is a non-toxic substance made from the ground up fossils of marine life and freshwater organisms.

Many benefits of this amazing powder include helping with joint pain. As we all know, when a pet is in pain, they really can't be bothered to go out for a walk. This is actually more harmful to them because they need to keep the joints moving as it helps the healing process. My fourteen year old dog can't be asked, but after a month of being on this she has improved and now wants to participate and meet other dogs again.

I'm not advocating that it's a miracle cure, as certain other factors and obviously a good diet are important, but I would certainly give it a try.

Dosage

Diatomaceous earth is very easily dissolved in water and I give my small dog a half teaspoon daily. I would give one teaspoon daily to larger dogs.

I have known for a while that **Turmeric spice** has been beneficial for my joint pain, but recently discovered when buying a new organic pet food that they are now adding it to dog food. One benefit is that it helps support new blood cell formation, essential when trying to repair damage to the joints and cartilage.

Turmeric plant

When I make turkey burgers I add turmeric and my two dogs love it.

Saphie and her boyfriend Winston

Bad Breath

Your pooch may not have the sweetest, kissable breath, but the expression "dog breath" does apply to canines as well as dogs. The solutions for curing it are very similar. If the breath is pungent most of the time it is either that they have old food stuck in between their teeth, or they could have a digestive problem like an upset stomach.

If you feel it is a digestive problem, sometimes it's due to their diet. Too much animal protein can produce gastrointestinal fermentation, the effects being that they produce gas from the rectum or a sour odour coming from the mouth. Check their gums. They could also be suffering from a case of Gingivitis or inflammation of the gums. A build-up of plaque is also a cause. This is a sticky bacterium that tends to accumulate on the teeth.

To eliminate your pet's bad breath, follow these simple daily tips.

Brushing teeth

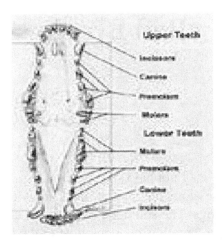

I know this is easier said than done because my dogs can make it difficult at times, but I try to make it as pleasant as possible. I bought a small finger brush because my dogs are a small size and I found it so much easier to gently massage the gums and teeth using also a small amount of pet paste. Never use human toothpaste on your dog. However clever you may think your pet is I do not think I have ever known a dog to rinse and spit out the contents after brushing.

Dogs love to play fetch and you could take advantage of this by finding a toy that acts like dental floss such as a rope or a chewy toy.

If you think the bad breath is being caused by a build-up of plaque, then a gentle wipe over the teeth with a small piece of gauze will help. My dogs love carrots. Giving your pooch carrots will act as a tooth scraper, taking away some of the stink causing plaque.

Pet spray

You can make your own spray from ingredients in your refrigerator, namely **Parsley**. Add several sprigs of parsley to hot water and allow it to stand until it has cooled off. If your dog will drink it, that's good, but if not, put contents into a spray bottle and gentle spray in the mouth.

Parsley

Coriander and Margosa leaves can be added to your dogs toothpaste or mouthwash as they naturally deal with the issue of bad breath. You can also allow them chew on some **peppermint leaves.**

Peppermint

Probiotics

I am a strong advocate of a good probiotic for helping with any digestive problem and if this is the cause of bad breath, then giving this to your dog will almost certainly help.

Papaya tablets assist in the digestion of food and are a good way to control halitosis. You can purchase these from any health food store. Crush one tablet and mix it with the pet's food. Papaya is good for breaking down food matter in the gut quickly. The enzymes released will stop excess gas, which in turn stop flatulence and bad breath.

Papaya Tree

If your dog is partial to biscuits, opt for the black ones. They contain charcoal and may not be as attractive as the pink or yellow ones, but the binding benefit of the charcoal will absorb bad odours effectively. Don't go overboard with them, though, as they can also bind essential nutrients, so just give one or two a day.

Lemons

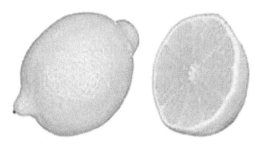

Squeezing a lemon into drinking water is another effective treatment of bad breath because it will cleanse his mouth and renew his palette. A word of caution: don't go overboard as he will just turn his nose up. Another important component in treating your pooch's bad breath is water. The germs present in the mouth need to be flushed out and an ideal way is to encourage them to drink more.

My dogs started to drink water off of the bedside cabinet as pups, so it is now a ritual every night that they drink water before bed. Maybe this is spoiling them, but at least I know they are getting their teeth flushed clean of food.

Brown rice

If your dog has bad breath and it seems to be from a digestive disorder not a dental issue, then mixing brown rice in with their diet helps digestion.

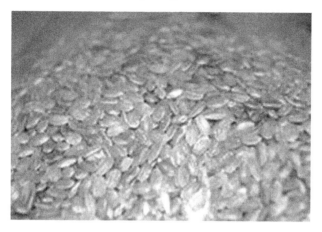

Behavioural Problems

Why do you love your furry housemates despite their behavioural problems?

Are you bothered by your pet's behavioural problems?

The key to helping your beloved pet is still in your hands.

You need to identify your personal or your family's reasons for wanting your dog around in order to seek ways to improve or eliminate any behavioural problems.

Some reasons why people love to have them around:

> The right pet helps people to feel socially confident.

> Some people are shy, but when they walk in public with their by their side, it can make all the difference.

> The ends up boosting that owner's confidence.

> These dogs help owners develop better personal characteristics.

Gone are the days of the stereotypical "crazy lady".

Have you noticed most owners are easy to connect with?

They are empathetic, sweet and tender people.

 reciprocate the love you give them.

In all our relationships, it helps to know, see and feel the affections we give are being reflected back on us.

We want to make sure that the objects of our love enjoy our company so we feel satisfied with the relationships we have with them.

So a wagging its tail can create this kind of a relationship with you and your family and it feels nurturing.

There are certain dogs which need your help to overcome behavioural problems.

It is not a question of whether you love your pet or do you love how your four-legged friend makes you feel. The important thing is that there is a need to address any behavioural problem in order to bring the joy back into your home.

It's such a wonderful thing that dogs and Animals can live together in one house. Here you can see that a dogs behaviour can be adorable and charming or hostile and disastrous.

They are part of the family and we always take care of our family. More often than not behavioural problems are issues in communication between the owner and the animal. Like most of our human relationships, they have special needs that must be met in order to behave well.

There are different reasons why a pet may become aggressive. One can be blamed for the territorial instinct, distress and defensiveness. They all contribute to the dog having an aggressive behavioural problem.

A dogs aggression is one of the most major behavioural problems any pet owner will experience, and can be as upsetting for the dog as it is for the whole family. Little do owners know, these types of aggression problems stem from a natural sense of dominance and canine experts say they need calm assertive leadership from you, the pet owner. You will need to learn and establish certain rules and limitations.

Another way to eliminate behavioural problems is to exercise your dog. Yes, exercise! A good walk burns the dogs extra energy and in turn helps in maintaining and calming the dogs state of mind.

To make it simple, dogs are part of our household, and our home relationships include them. Learning how to earn their trust, loyalty and respect can solve most, if not all, of their behavioural problems.

Diet

It is important that your dog has a natural, preservative-free or allergy diet, as their behaviour could be an intolerance to certain foods or additives.

Oats

Oats

As I have previously stated, oats have a calming effect and can be made into porridge. Try adding some raw honey, or a brewer's yeast vitamin; these are anti-stress supplements.

Many of the recommendations for anxiety can also be used.

Bladder Problems

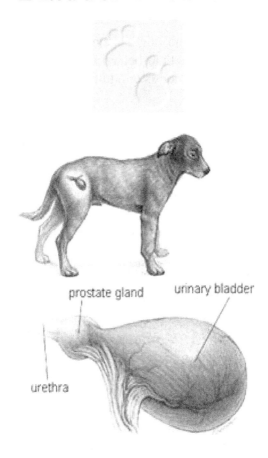

prostate gland   urinary bladder

urethra

Before we go down the route of giving your any alternative therapy for a bladder problem, let's look at the symptoms to watch out for:

- Fever, backache, lethargy

- Changes in the colour of the urine such as bloody or darker than normal

- Change in the odour

- Pain when passing urine

- Problems during urination

- Constant licking of the genitals

- Passing very little or no urine

Causes could be related to poor diet, stress, a fungal infection, bladder stones, tumours or an injury.

A lot has been said about diet being the cause for some bladder problems. Dry commercial foods are a major culprit in producing alkaline urine and they are the worst type of diet for your dog to be on as they rob the system of any moisture. If you are aware that this may be the cause then immediately change your pet's food to a high quality canned food or a homemade diet. This is not as difficult as it seems, sometimes mixing raw vegetables in can help.

Once you have detected any one of the above signs or symptoms, get advice from your vet and see if it's possible to treat with alternative or homoeopathic remedies.

Your vet may insist that your pet be treated with antibiotics which won't always kill the bacteria, just make them go away for a while, so it is important to look at the long term options.

Some pet stores are aware of the natural ways to treat animals and do sell certain products especially for bladder problems which are entirely safe, ones to look for are:

Catharis C6

Staphysagris C6

BerberisVulgaris

Uva Ursi (Bearberry)

Uva Ursi (Bearberry)

Cranberry

All of the above products have been tested and have been proven to, not only improve your pets urinary health but contain properties that are beneficial in the overall wellbeing and long term health of your .

You must encourage your to drink plenty as the more they do, the more they will urinate, thus flushing the bacteria out of the bladder. Keeping your dog hydrated is essential in treating this problem.

Juniper berry is an herb known for increasing the rate the kidneys can filter out impurities, and thus will increase the urine output. This works very well in treating severe urinary tract infections.

Juniper berry

Uva Ursi is one of the most powerful natural astringents available. Many Holistic veterinarians use it to attack a whole range of pathogens that are normally the cause of many UTIs. It has been known to reduce the inflammation associated with these infections and to stop any bleeding.

Echinacea tincture is often recommended for an acute infection and is useful in treating UTIs

Echinacea

Horsetail is useful if you see blood in the urine with any infections.

Marshmallow root works really well when there is inflammation in the urinary tract. It stimulates the immune system, thus attacking the bacteria, whilst also having a soothing effect on the body and reducing any irritation.

Marshmallow root

Cranberry or blueberry prevents the bacteria from attaching to the lining of the urinary tract to prevent recurring infections

Cranberry

Do not treat the idea that your pet may have a urinary tract infection lightly. If untreated, it can develop into something more serious and the quicker you can get a diagnosis from your veterinarian, the quicker you can treat holistically.

If you purchase any of the above remedies there will be dosage instructions. If not, please ask a professional for help.

Sometimes when your pet has a UTI they can become incontinent. If this is happening because of the infection, the incontinence will stop once this is treated. On the other hand, if they also have an incontinence problem then we will have to treat that afterwards.

Symptoms of Incontinence:

- Infection of the Bladder or urinary tract infection (as suggested)

- Bladder Stones

- Excessive consumption of water

- Weak Bladder Sphincter

- Spinal cord damage or disease

One of the most common causes of incontinence, especially in the spayed female, is a weak sphincter muscle in the bladder. This is due to having a low oestrogen level and can happen any time after the female dog has been spayed. Males can also develop this but typically affects older dogs. Another reason to keep your dog fit is because, if they develop obesity, it contributes to a weakened bladder sphincter.

If your female dog has been diagnosed with this problem, they normally respond well to hormone treatments. The natural supplement to give in this case is soy isoflavones or any other herbs that provide phytoestrogens or glandular extracts; these are useful in treating incontinence. In some cases, changing to a raw freeze-dried or grain-free diet has been known to cure incontinence.

It is always best to seek help from a professional for other causes of incontinence.

Barney watching the birds!

Bowel and Digestive Disorders

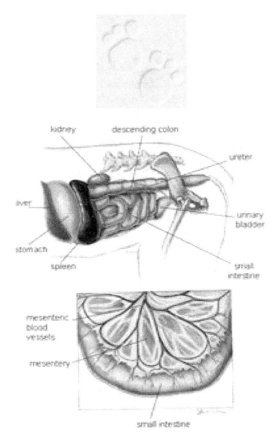

Many veterinarians say that the most common problem they see is Gastrointestinal upset and this is often related to a food allergy.

Owners present there dog to the vet with a range of symptoms including:

- Vomiting and diarrhoea

- Trapped wind or gas

- Constipation

- Loss of appetite

- Difficulty swallowing

- Change in the stools

- Grey stools may indicate liver problems

- Black stools may indicate bleeding in the upper part of tract

Although dogs have the same components as humans, they differ in how they are used. Teeth in the animal are not needed to chew, they are used to cut and crush before swallowing the food into the stomach which ultimately takes care of the digestion process. We need saliva to break down our food using the enzymes present. A dog doesn't. It only needs the saliva to lubricate the act of swallowing so it can easily pass through the oesophagus on its way to the stomach.

Compared to the human stomach, a dog can take up to 70-75% of the full capacity, which is why it is possible to feed your animal once a day. If you do feed twice a day, you have to give smaller amounts. It can also take up to twenty-four hours for a dog to properly digest a meal.

Diarrhoea

This is by far the most common ailment seen by pet owners, but there are many remedies that can be given at home from the first onset of the problem. Diarrhoea is defined when the stools passed are runny or loose in consistency, and more frequent than normal. It can sometimes be accompanied by mucus or blood, which can be an indication that the pet has a more serious complaint called Colitis.

To help protect the mucus membranes of the intestinal tract after a bout of Diarrhoea, you can give **Slippery Elm.**

Slippery Elm Tree

Tree Bark powder is good for acute intestinal disorders and can be given during and after periods of diarrhoea. It helps the system get back to its normal function. At the first onset of any change in my dog and his normal motion I give tree bark accompanied by probiotic powder. This seems to settle it down.

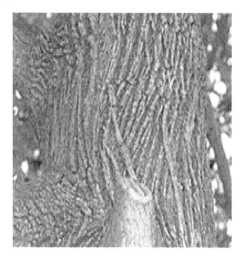

Tree Bark

Dosage

The dosage is one teaspoon twice a day for small dogs. For medium and larger dogs, give two teaspoons twice a day until the diarrhoea has ceased.

Organic yoghurt is a healthy treat for your pet. It contains live acidophilus which helps the good bacteria in the gut stay balanced and keeps the bad bacteria away.

I watched a TV program about various alternative therapies people had tried at home that they felt benefited them, and a panel of three doctors had to decide if they thought it worked or not.

A lady in her sixties had been suffering for many years with Crohn's disease, a very painful and severely debilitating gastric condition. She had heard about Tree Bark through internet research and decided to give it a go. She went to her local woods and scraped some healthy looking tree bark from a tree, took it home and soaked it in hot water making a tea. Within a couple of weeks this ladies symptoms had alleviated so much she decided to make it a way of life. She found tree bark powder and stopped all her medication. She was instantly dismissed on television by this panel as saying it was probably due to her not being as stressed.

This dismissive attitude of so-called intelligent people only makes me even more determined to prove them wrong. There are natural alternatives out there that help, and we have to find and pass on the knowledge so many more pet owners will benefit.

If the pet has been given antibiotics by the vet as a last resort, then acidophilus will keep any yeast infection at bay, which is a side effect of taking them. For more serious cases of diarrhoea, you can also give **Cankur** which contains **Kaolin and Pectin**. This acts as a binding agent against the harmful bacteria and toxins in the gut and successfully removes them. Cankur does have a probiotic in it as well, which is essential in keeping the gut healthy.

To also stop Diarrhoea in Animals you can mix and give them the following every three to four hours:

1 cup of cooked white rice with ¼ cup of coconut milk

For small dogs give– 1-2 Tablespoons every 3-4 hours

Medium size dogs– ½ cup every 3-4 hours

Large dogs– 1 cup every 3-4 hours

If after one or two days the diarrhoea seems to be getting better and it appears the stools are harder, then you can slowly add boiled chicken or beef with some white rice.

If the diarrhoea contains blood or your pet really does not seem well enough for you to try any home remedies, immediately take him to the vet. All home remedies are a guideline and a first response to more professional help, but many times can be treated at home.

If your pet has been suffering from a bout of diarrhoea, they need to replenish their fluids. A good way to do this is to find a good electrolyte flavourless supplement to get the fluid balance back on track, especially if they have also been vomiting because they may be dehydrated.

Another way to hydrate your pet is to give **coconut water** or **coconut juice** every two hours. The amount will depend on their size, so start with 5mls for small dogs and up to 40mls for larger dogs.

When many athletes have been running long distances or working out at the gym, they tend to go for coconut water as a good way to rehydrate.

Always consult your veterinarian over the phone for the correct dosage.

Gas and Bloating

This can be a problem also, but can easily be corrected. If your pet has gas and bloating it's normally a sign of imbalances with the bacteria that live in the colon. We need good bacteria alive in the bowel to fight off infections, but sometimes due to a change of diet the stress can affect it. Try to avoid foods you think may have upset your dog . The major sources are carbohydrates and vegetables, so it is really down to the elimination process. A good herbal remedy containing a probiotic will soon settle the problem.

If you can get your pet to drink chamomile tea, this will certainly settle any gas or trapped wind causing colic pain in the tummy and will also help if the pet is anxious because of it.

Charcoal Biscuits can help reduce flatulence in dogs. Try to avoid foods that contain soybean, which is in some commercial foods. Soybean reacts with the bacteria in the gut and causes excess gas, flatulence and subsequently, bloating.

Charcoal

I find with a lot of the medication I give, the best way is to crush it on a spoon, mix with yoghurt, and place on the tongue of the dog. I use a syringe (without a needle) for liquids and gently administer in the side of the dogs mouth.

Constipation

This condition is as common in dogs as it is with us humans, especially as the pet becomes older. It can develop quickly and if it's not monitored correctly, it can become something more severe like a blockage.

The inevitable happens and they will need to be seen by a vet to either have an enema, which is not a pleasant experience, or surgery in some cases. Hopefully though, if you are vigilant and look for the first signs of the problem, you can avoid a trip to the vet's office.

Watch for hard faeces or pain when trying to go, swelling of the abdomen or bloating, mucus or sometimes blood in the stool, the colour of the stool may be darker than usual, appetite loss and listlessness. They will just look at you when it's time to go out for a walk. They can also smell a little gassy. The above drastic treatments hopefully can be avoided if you watch out for the above tell-tale signs that something is not quite right.

Constipation can be caused by your pet being dehydrated, so always check their fluid intake. Here's a trick I have if you feel they are not drinking enough. Run a tap near them and change the water bowl frequently. If you have an older dog they are more prone to constipation as they start to become inactive. Getting them out for exercise is a must, and giving them Salmon fish oil. It acts as a lubricant and will keep the faeces soft, and they will start to have the feeling back in the bowel again. If you have a pet like mine, and they for some reason like to pick up and eat tissues, then any foreign object could block the bowel. Always make sure that does not happen when out on your daily walks.

You can sprinkle **Psyllium husk powder** on their food. It is a bulk-forming laxative that will make the bowel work. When giving this, always watch the fluid intake. Not enough water could make the faeces bulkier, but also harder. You can make a meat and vegetable broth and mix the Psyllium husk powder in it.

Psyllium Husks

Canned pumpkin will soften the stools and is a good source of fibre. A tablespoon or two daily for a few days added to their food is sufficient.

Green vegetables can be mashed in with their food or mixed with coconut oil. I have tried this and have also hand fed my a small amount and he actually quite liked it and seemed to work well for him.

I have used **Cider Vinegar** for many years for my joints, but know it also benefits the bowel. It improves the digestion of any pet, and if they happen to have arthritis as well, it will help that also. You can give one half teaspoon to small dogs and one teaspoon to medium or large dogs once a day. It is not pleasant to taste, so you can add a small amount of honey and dilute in a small amount of water.

If you need a non-prescription medication, **Lactulose** is available online from a reputable pet pharmacy. As with dogs, it will soften the faeces. It is synthetic and sugar-based and will promote peristalsis (bowel movements) naturally through the intestines.

Milk will cause diarrhoea in , but the flipside is that if given to a constipated pet, a little will provide the relief they need. Offer a half cup morning and night and it should do the trick.

Liquid Paraffin works the same way, softening the stools and allowing for easier movement. **Ginger** is well known to help with dogs who suffer from digestive problems, and it helps with constipation.

Ginger also helps if your pet has inflammation in the bowel and will reduce any muscle spasms they may be experiencing because of being constipated. It is also good if they are feeling sick or nauseous. The taste is obviously not very pleasant like many of the remedies I have recommended, but you have to be smart and place directly on the dogs tongue or with their favourite food or treats.

Ginger

Bran is a good fibre to treat constipation and a daily sprinkle on food will help.

If you ever feel that your pet needs laxatives because the constipation is too severe to be treated at home, please do not try and get an enema or suppositories online. If they are not administered properly, these can cause more damage to your pet. It is best you try any of the home remedies I have suggested first and then please visit your local vet. They are experienced and will be able to diagnose a more serious problem.

Worms and parasites

Worms can be a big problem for some and the earliest signs to look out for are diarrhoea–it could be bloody, weight loss, gas, gastrointestinal pain, vomiting and you may see worms in the vomit. Your pet could also have worms, but not be experiencing any symptoms.

The most common type of worm for adult dogs is the **tapeworm.** These are parasites that have a small head with many tiny egg-filled segments attached and have been known to grow several inches and, in extreme cases up to a foot. They attach themselves to the intestinal tract.

Dogs get these types of worms from fleas, so it is always very important to treat your pet when you see the first sign of any flea infestation.

Another way to avoid your pet catching these is to keep them away from any dead wild life. I recently found a dead young fox in my garden and fortunately was quick enough to remove it before my two dogs became exposed. One tell-tale sign that they may have a tapeworm is they scoot around the floor with their rear end rubbing. Always check your pet's stools if you suspect they have a tapeworm. You will often see segments that look like grains of rice.

There are many products out there from your vet to treat fleas and worms, but if you opt for an alternative, I have listed a few for you.

Probiotics are healthy bacteria for the intestines. They will eat away at the worm's outer coating until they release their hold on the intestinal walls.

Give your one non-dairy capsule of an acidophilus probiotic with every meal. Another positive for introducing a probiotic is that it will aid the absorption of essential nutrients.

I have suggested *Diatomaceous earth* for other problems with your pet, but this is also an excellent product to kill internal parasites. This is a non-toxic substance made from the ground-up fossils of freshwater organisms. It is a fine powder and is easily absorbed with fluid or sprinkled on food. It is tasteless so your pet will not suspect anything! The reason this product works so well with parasites is because the powder is composed of sharp-edged particles. These are deadly to worms because they break through the protective coating of the larvae making it dehydrate and die. These sharp edges do not harm dogs or people. When buying this product always choose a *food-grade* diatomaceous earth product. Any other type, especially ones used for gardening, can be harmful to your pet.

To eliminate worms and parasites, give a half teaspoon to dogs 10kg or under, and increase to one teaspoon for dogs over and up to 25kg.

Garlic

Garlic

We have known this product helps with digestive problems for a long time and now we can use it to get rid of worms. Garlic contains sulphur compounds and other good nutrients such as Allicin and Alliin that are of good medicinal value–all being natural antibiotics and a perfect immune system booster.

Dosage

One clove of garlic either crushed or minced added to your pet's food throughout the day, normally in four to six portions.

This should be increased to two or three cloves daily for larger dogs.

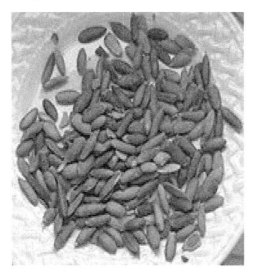

Pumpkin seeds

We have discovered how good **pumpkin seeds** are for any digestive disorder, and the same applies to worms. They are a traditional remedy for roundworms and tapeworms. What makes this such a good worm fighter? It contains an amino acid called Cucurbitin, which has anti-worm properties and works by paralyzing and eliminating worms in the digestive tract.

If you give ground pumpkins seeds you also give your pet the added bonus of having protein, calcium, zinc, potassium and fibre, all important minerals for your pet's health.

Carrots can be used to eliminate worms and any other internal parasite because the carrot scrapes the mucus off the walls of the intestines where the parasite is living. For one week add grated carrot to your dogs food each morning. It will take a few days to work, so be patient. Repeat again in a few weeks.

Parsley will safely treat worms in your dog. Mix a handful of fresh parsley in a blender and then cook with a small amount of water for at least three minutes. Remove the water by straining and freeze into ice cubes and then add an ice cube to your dogs water.

Parsley

Wormwood

This herb has a long history as a good fix for intestinal worms. This contains a substance called sesquiterpene lactones, which have been shown to weaken the membrane of the worm. You should only give your pet a small amount of this product weekly, as too much could possibly cause problems with your pet's kidneys or liver.

Wormwood

You can also combine ground pumpkin seeds with wheat germ oil.

Use one quarter teaspoon of wheat germ oil with one quarter teaspoon of ground pumpkin seeds for every ten to twenty pounds of your pet's weight. For dogs under this weight, give half the dosage.

If you want a simple but effective way to eliminate worms or parasites, try putting your dog on a twenty-four hour fast once a week. Doing this will expel the worms and stop them from returning. Worms need food to survive, so if you are depriving them of food they will become weak and they will be cleared out of the digestive system.

Again, always consult your vet if you wish to fast your dog especially if he is old or not in the best of health.

Ear and Eye Complaints

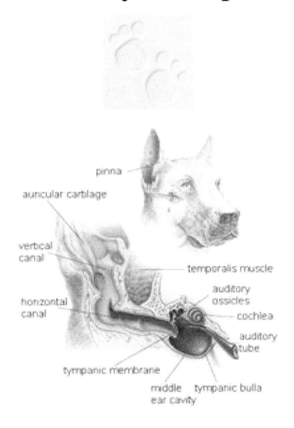

pinna

auricular cartilage

vertical canal

horizontal canal

temporalis muscle

auditory ossicles

cochlea

auditory tube

tympanic membrane

middle ear cavity

tympanic bulla

Ear Discharges

Ear problems can be very common for a dog and cover many complaints such as ear mites, wax, smelly ears discharge, infection or inflammation.

Ear mites seem to be the most common and like to live in the ear canal of an animal, causing irritation and a thick brownish crust. Your pet will shake his head vigorously and try to head scratch. They will feel like they have an ear full of jumping beans and when it is severe, they will scratch so much that they can make the area raw and a skin infection will follow.

If you have other Animals in the household it is more than likely they are also infected, as it is generally passed from animal to animal. They can be successfully treated but you will need to be patient and persevere.

Treatment

You will need mineral oil and a small dropper to deposit a few drops of the oil into the ear canal and leave for a few hours. We need to do this to soften the crusts that have formed. After a few hours, use an ear-cleaning syringe and put equal portions of lukewarm distilled water and white vinegar and gently flush any debris from the ear canal. Please do not use too much pressure as it is painful for the animal, so gently squeeze, release, and squeeze. After a while, gently use cotton inside the ear and try to remove any loose gunk.

You can repeat this process as often as you feel your animal can tolerate it until the area is clean. If you use a torch, you can see inside much easier. If they have been scratching a lot, it is likely they will need a drop or two of baby oil to soothe them. Heat the oil slightly and use enough to just the coat the ear canal.

Another remedy to soothe the itch of ear mites is garlic and olive oil.

Crush four cloves of garlic then place them in a cup of olive oil. Allow the mixture to stand overnight, sieve the oil and discard the crushed garlic. Heat the oil until it is just lukewarm and then put several drops into the ear canal.

As well as smothering the ear mites, the combination is very soothing for the animal. This can be used daily or on alternate days, depending on the severity of the condition.

A regime of cleaning your pet's ears is always a good thing, and hopefully will prevent further infestations. You can use a cotton swab dipped in hydrogen peroxide to gently clean out the canal. Avoid going in too deeply, if you cannot see the cotton tip you have gone too far.

Sometimes we get it wrong and misdiagnose the cause of itching in our pet's as mites when, in fact, it is something different like a yeast infection. Many veterinarians regard allergies as being the underlying cause that triggers a yeast infection, and they must be treated on a regular basis.

Acidophilus is a friendly strain bacteria that will help you fight a fungal or yeast infection. I purchased a powder online and I keep it for many different ailments. You can use any good natural pet ear cleaning products and gently clean the ear. You could also use water in a cup, add one ounce of vinegar and flush the ears out the same as if treating ear mites. They will shake the ears many times afterwards, but that's a good thing as it gets rid of any excess. Put a pinch of acidophilus powder into one ounce of water. Using a dropper, squirt into the ear making sure it goes down deep enough.

The acidophilus will cleanse the ear and remove any nasty bacteria and yeast lurking there. You have to repeat this procedure periodically as the ear canal is not a normal habitat for acidophilus and it will need to be replaced.

You will notice the difference in the discharge from the ear if it is a bacterial infection. It is normally gooey looking, with pus sometimes. Whereas yeast infections can always be identified by a strong odour similar to a human's smelly feet, and the presence of lots of dark brown sticky wax.

If you do not see any improvement after one month, or you notice a rash or they have a painful irritation, I recommend you see a vet. They may have to prescribe something stronger.

Eye Disorders

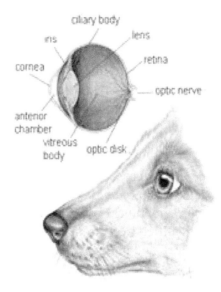

Because our dogs don't depend on sight as much as we do, they could be running around quite happily for many years without you realizing there is a problem that needs to be diagnosed.

It is easy to spot the first signs and symptoms of a problem. A classic example is a red and blood-shot eye. This could be the first sign that glaucoma is present, which is when the pressure in the eye increases. They can also develop something called dry eye, which is another serious condition as the eye does not have a normal covering of tears. If they have this condition they invariably have pus in the eyeball and will have to visit a veterinarian as with the more serious eye conditions like glaucoma.

More commonly seen is a condition called conjunctivitis, which is inflammation around the white of the eye and the lining of the eyelid, and can be treated at first with alternative remedies. The eyes become red, sore and swollen and can make your pet's eyes itchy with an abundance of either pus or tears. It is often associated with allergies or some type of minor irritation and it not usually serious, but should not be left untreated.

Treatments

With a soft clean cotton ball or a cloth soaked in lukewarm water, squeeze out any excess and gently wipe away any discharge from the eyes. Repeat this twice a day as this is the first step to stopping any progression of the infection.

You can buy over the counter eye scrubs from any pet shop, the difference in using this is that it is pH-balanced so will cause less stinging.

You need to focus on the inside of the eye, so it is important to keep the lid clean. You can do this by buying some artificial tears, which will help wash away any particles that may be the cause of the problem.

Pampering your pet even further is to use a wet cloth soaked again in lukewarm water, wring it out, and sit and cuddle your dog with the cloth over the eyes for about five minutes. It makes them feel better and aids the recovery of keeping the eyes clean. You can also add a few drops of **chamomile essences** to the water.

Chamomile

To enhance the healing process, a tea can be made from **goldenseal** to bathe the eyes the same way, but also add Vitamin E. Another alternative is a pad soaked with **Witch hazel** over the eyes. These remedies will soothe, calm and promote the healing process.

There is a connection with the liver and the eyes and many therapists believe that cleansing and nourishing the liver will usually help with chronic eye conditions that have not responded to conventional medicines and treatments.

I know well the benefits of liver detoxifications from my position as a Colonic therapist and have always recommended **milk thistle** between colonics. You can also add **glutamine**, an amino acid essential for nourishing the intestinal tract, which will ease the burden on the liver.

Milk Thistle

Dosage it is always advisable to give supplements with meals.

Glutamine: *500 milligrams twice a day for all Animals*

Milk thistle: *250 to 500 milligrams twice a day for dogs, this depends on the size of the animal and how severe the condition is.*

Once you have started treating your with various remedies, it is very important that you stop them from rubbing the eyes. They will be runny and itchy and a dogs natural instinct is to find the nearest carpet and rub over it. I have a collar from a pet shop, but if you do not, most vets will have them in stock. They don't like it, but it will prevent further problems occurring.

Home Health Check

As a qualified nurse I am at an advantage in noticing if I am sick, but with a dog you do not need medical knowledge if you follow a simple checklist.

It is not an easy task to know if our pet is sick, because they are more robust than say a pet cat.. They could have a cracked tooth and still be chewing and playing with a toy. So by going through a home check, you will be able to spot the early signs of a problem or a sickness before they escalate into a much bigger one.

Again, I am not advocating the elimination of your vet being able to diagnose illnesses, but in truth we only normally take them for routine visits maybe once or twice a year. You are the one that can see the small signs that all is not well through their daily habits. You can incorporate the check into playtime quite easily, and they will not even be aware they are being examined.

The Ears

Dogs have a high risk and are prone to ear infections because of the position of the inner tube–it slants downwards and ends where a horizontal tube begins. This is designed to protect the ear from injuries, but the down side is it allows debris, leaves and wax to become trapped which is a sure breeding ground for infections.

As well as looking at the colour and texture of the ear, use your sense of smell to detect any odour. If you notice any, it could be the first sign of an infection. The ear should be glossy, smooth and odourless. It should have a slight sheen from the natural oil inside and the skin colour should be pale pink. If you see a dark waxy build up with no odour, it just means they need a good cleaning so try one of my listed remedies in the ear section.

If your dog seems dizzy and continually wants to scratch or shake the head, this is a sure sign that something is wrong with the inner ear. If the alternative remedies for cleaning are not working, please take the animal to the vet straight away.

The Eyes should be bright with the centre being clear. Both pupils should be the same size and be sure to check under the lids. The tissue should be a nice healthy looking pink colour. Depending on what breed you have, some dogs do have a blackish tinge on the pink membrane so it's nothing to be worried about as that's normal.

Infection will be easy to spot as you will see either yellow or green pus coming from the eye. Some dogs are prone to produce more tears, especially smaller ones like Pekinese or pugs because their eyes bulge. So although they look like they are weeping excessively, it is the way the tear canal is shaped.

If your does seem to be weeping too much it could be due to an allergy, or if it is watery and is accompanied by redness, then perhaps something is stuck in the eye. Never try to physically remove anything you see, this needs to be done by a vet.

I have noticed over the years my fourteen year old dogs eyes are changing. As she ages, they seem to be taking on a bluish tinge. If this was also accompanied by a cloudy cast and silver flecks, then this could be hardening of the lens which suggests cataracts. If the eye is bluish and blood-shot or is painful, this is a sign of glaucoma which is a serious condition. Like dogs, it affects the pressure in the eye and if left untreated, could cause blindness. Some breeds like Bassett hounds or cocker spaniels are more prone to glaucoma.

Mouth and teeth

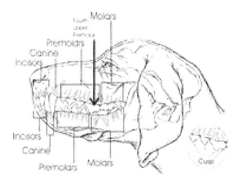

Check all the teeth and gums. Gums should be pink and they should have a nice set of forty-two white teeth! The breath should be sweet and not offensive when they want to snuggle into your face.

Although most dogs don't like their mouths being opened, it is important to do this on a regular basis, at least once or twice a week. In the long term you will be avoiding many problems in the future.

Nose

It is not true that if a dogs nose is warm they must be sick. As long as it is moist without cracks, they are healthy. There should not be any discharge or change in the pigmentation.

Body and Limbs

Run your fingers along the spine of your dog, and proceed to the chest and abdomen using only slight pressure, your dog should not be showing any signs of pain. Lift a leg one by one and check for any swelling, lumps, sores, or other changes. Check to see if he is hunching or the posture is rigid.

Heart rate for dogs can vary. Anything from 60 to 150 beats per minute can depend on the size of the dog. Larger dogs have a bigger heart but have a slower heart rate than a smaller dog. If you are unsure about your own pet you can always check with your veterinarian.

If you want to check your 's heart rate, the best place to do this is by finding the femoral artery which runs along the thigh bone inside the hind leg, about halfway between the hip and the knee. You will feel a groove between the muscles and that is the area to place your fingers. Do not use your thumb as this has its own strong pulse. Count the number of beats for fifteen seconds and multiply this by four. That is how you calculate the beats per minute.

Lungs: The best way to check the respiratory system of your dog is to use your ears. If they are breathing normally, you will not notice anything is wrong. Normal breathing for a dog when they are resting or sleeping is between ten to thirty breaths per minute. If you notice the breathing is rapid whilst they are sleeping, it is not normal and it is best to get them checked out.

Circulation is easy to check on your dog. Lift up the dogs lip from the side, press gently on the gum by the sharp canine tooth, when you stop pressing you will either notice that the pale spot returns to being a healthy pink when released after a couple of seconds, or if it remains pale then your pet could have circulation problems.

To take your dog's temperature, you will need a rectal thermometer and the use of someone else's hands to hold your dogs head and shoulders. This isn't nice for them and they will resist, but a few kind and calming words will help while you slide it in using some type of petroleum jelly.

Leave it in for two to three minutes to get a good reading and gently wipe the anus area with a tissue after removing. A dogs normal temperature ranges from 99.5 to 102.5F. If it's the higher end, we would feel they have a fever. My dog had a reading of 104.F and did have an infection, but it was not life threatening and only lasted for a few days.

The Home Check is only a guideline for you to keep an eye on your pets health, which will hopefully make you aware of any changes that may be occurring, giving you first response in any treatment.

It is not intended that if you discover anything serious you should refrain from visiting the vet because of wanting to try alternative remedies. It is always best for your peace of mind to get a professional opinion and then you can decide if you want to go down the conventional or alternative route.

Obesity

It is too easy to overdose our dogs on kindness by giving them treats. It is a natural thing because we love them, but obesity in dogs is rising. A few surveys estimate that between twenty and forty percent of dogs are now obese.

One of the biggest barriers for owners is to actually admit that they have allowed their pets to become overweight or obese. To check if your dog is overweight, stand over them looking down. You should see a well-defined waistline below the rib cage and above the hips. You should also place both of your hands on your dogs ribcage, press down and you should be able to feel the individual ribs.

Older dogs do tend to gain weight because their metabolisms slow down, so you should compensate this with changing their diet.

Neutering and other factors

Some pet owners are concerned that once their is spayed or neutered, they will automatically put on weight.

This is not the case. In some instances dogs have gained weight, but this is due to a combination of factors: Eating too many calories, a slow metabolic rate, hormonal changes and insufficient exercise.

If you pay attention to your dog's diet and exercise them at least once a day, this will prevent weight gain after the pet has been spayed or neutered.

The food you buy is irrelevant in how fat your dog is becoming. It is all about how much you are feeding them, and the giving of too many treats.

As well as causing discomfort to your dog obesity will contribute and exacerbate other diseases such as:

- High Blood Pressure

- Diabetes

- Poor Quality food

- Heart or lung Disease

- Difficulty Breathing

- More discomfort for arthritic dogs

- Constipation, Liver disease

- Risk under anaesthesia

- Abnormal life expectancy

• Generally have more susceptibility to developing tumours

If your pet is showing signs of being overweight, it's time to feed him less, but more often. Don't put your dog on a crash diet, there is no need. Start by reducing his intake by twenty percent, he will probably notice but you can feed him a smaller amount later.

Special food designed specifically for weight loss will be lower in fat but contain more fibre, essential for filling your out, and as fibre contains very little calories will help your lose weight. Even though they are meat eaters, dogs love carrots and I don't think they mind having vegetables added to their diet now and then.

The treats they have gotten used to must be trimmed down in order for them to lose weight. You can buy low-calorie biscuits and break them into small pieces so they think they are getting more than they actually are.

If you still need to feed your dog commercial pet food, please check for one that contains low fat and high quality protein and carbohydrates. On average, most pet foods have a fat content of roughly sixteen percent. A low fat alternative will only contain ten percent and enhance the wellbeing of your dog while on a weight loss program.

The main home remedies for your have everything to do with his diet and it is important to prepare as many meals containing low fat but good for them protein. They include:

- Chicken or turkey breast

- Ground Beef, fat removed after cooking

- Fish containing essential Omega 3 fatty acids will help with arthritis in older dogs

- Low fat dairy such as cheese or plain yoghurt

- Eggs

Eggs are a good source of protein, but be careful on how many egg yolks you give as they are also high in fat.

I make a turkey mince loaf with:

- *Turkey*

- *Grated carrots*

- *Coriander*

- *Chopped broccoli*

- *Green peas*

- *Bind with 2 eggs*

I usually make two loaves, one for me and one for the dogs. I slice it up and freeze for later. They especially love it if I add a touch of gravy.

We have mentioned diet to control obesity, but exercise plays an important part in the fight to rid any excess pounds your dog has. To maintain a lean body, you need to keep up a good exercise regime. It is not good enough to just leave your dog in the back garden playing with balls, digging up holes, and occasionally going mad if a fox happens to invade his territory. I believe a dog also needs to socialize with other dogs in the park or, in my case, down on the beach. They like nothing more than running along the water's edge looking for different items to play with.

If it is not possible because of work commitments to go twice a day, then at least go for one long walk a day. It is not always possible to go every day if your dog is older. I have a seven year old and a fourteen year old and my pace is slower for the older dog, but I know by being persistent the older one benefits from even a short walk. Her weight is well under control and, as I have mentioned before, her joints will not become stiff and sore. She normally sleeps the rest of the day, but it is worth it.

If you can, allow your dog to go in the water. Swimming is a really good exercise for them, especially if they have arthritis.

Natural remedies to help with obesity

Various supplements can be used to help with any dietary and exercise program.

Chromium picolinate

This mineral is very helpful for dogs that have diabetes. It promotes the activity of insulin and its usefulness in fighting excess weight has been suggested.

Dandelion

This garden weed is used as a mild diuretic to support liver function and to help weight loss. It is rich in vitamins A, C, E, and the B complex group and is also a good source of calcium and potassium.

Dosage

The easiest way this tincture can be administered is by dropper.

Normally five to ten drops per ten pounds of your dogs weight is given two to three times daily.

If you want to double check the dosage of any herbal medicine, look it up in the "Herbal Doses for Dogs" book or check with your vet.

Tooth and Tartar problems

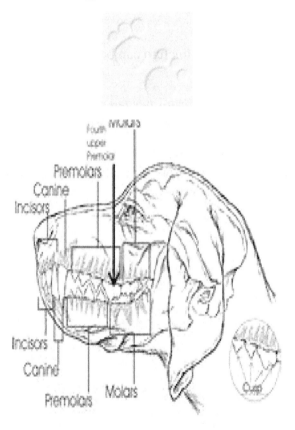

The lack of routine dental care is one of the main reasons vets see Animals with periodontal problems. A few minutes a day spent cleaning your pets teeth on a regular basis will keep them clean and healthy.

do not normally like toothbrushes and I found a solution. Try to get a hold of something called cotton tubaquaze. It is used with an applicator to bandage fingers. Put a small amount on your finger and apply the toothpaste to it. You can massage and clean the teeth gently and your pet will get used to the taste and touch of this daily routine. If they are happy with this, you can progress to a soft toothbrush. I find a toothbrush, especially on smaller dogs, quite cumbersome.

To get your pet used to having his teeth brushed, firstly get him used to the idea by gently massaging the lips with your finger in a circular motion. Do this for thirty to sixty seconds a day and continue for a few weeks. They will eventually feel comfortable with you and hopefully allow you to progress to the teeth and gums.

If the pooch feels comfortable, you can then progress to dog toothpaste or make a paste from baking soda and water. Be sure to put a little on their lips to allow them to get used to a strange taste. You will hopefully be able to brush those pearlies on a daily basis without ever having to lose any fingers!

To brush the teeth, put the gauze-wrapped finger or brush at a forty-five degree angle and start to clean in small circular motions, working one area at a time, lifting the lip if necessary. Teeth that touch the cheek are the ones to concentrate most on as they normally show more signs of tartar. After going in a circular motion with the brushing, finally do a downward stroke and this will remove it. Once you have mastered this technique and your pooch doesn't do a runner when he sees the brush coming towards him, this procedure can be done two or three times a week.

The two most common problems severe enough to visit the vet's office are gingivitis and periodontal disease. Gingivitis is inflammation of the gums. It can be reversed and, if caught in time, will not develop into a more serious condition called periodontal disease. This is a painful infection between the tooth and gums that can result in tooth loss if untreated and can spread infection to the rest of the body. I cannot stress enough how important it is to watch for any early signs, as the last thing you want is for your pet to be subjected to an anaesthetic. Simple cleaning each day is a necessity.

Signs of teeth and gum problems:

- Red swollen gums that may bleed when touched

- Sensitive to you touching face or mouth

- Runny nose and sneezing

- Excessive salivation

- Inability to eat properly and weight loss

- Swelling below eyes or on cheeks

- Sneezing or runny nose

- Loose or decayed teeth

- Yellow or brown plaque on teeth

- Bad breath – normally a sign of gum disease

These are just a few things to watch out for, but the main one is redness and tartar that looks like it is developing over the gums and top of teeth.

How many times has your pet wanted a cuddle and tried to lick your face? This is all very well until the smell coming from their breath is too much to bear! Pet Halitosis can be helped by a few home remedies found in your kitchen cupboard.

If you give your pet chicken for lunch or dinner add some brown rice. Good digestion plays an important part in healthy teeth and breath, and whole grains will help do this.

Carrot or Apple will remove plaque. Instead of giving biscuit treats after a meal, offer them a carrot or a piece of apple to chew on. My dogs love carrots, but is not that keen on apple. One out of two is okay!

Parsley

For good breath, break off a few sprigs of parsley and soak them in hot water until cool. Remove the parsley and either let your pet drink the water or spray a little into their mouth. I guarantee better breath when they decide to do all that licking and kissing again!

Parsley

Skin and Coat Conditions

Care and maintenance of the skin and coat

Skin and the coat of Animals that appear to be gifted with lustre, are such a joy and a goal of all pet owners.

How do you know that your most loved pets are truly healthy? Let's just say you know them so well that when someone asks you what makes them look so healthy you say, "Look at the skin and the coat."

Some diseases hide away past the skin and the coat, but an unhealthy looking outward appearance will tell you they need extra care in order to maintain optimum health.

Different dogs need different grooming regimes. As owners, you need to discover which one is best for your pet. Yes! Like parents to their children, a responsible pet owner must exhibit the same commitment and love. Like humans, our four-legged friends need help in order to prevent dull and lifeless coats.

Top priority is good nutrition and a balanced diet. They need red meat and a good amount of protein. We discuss further along that a normal diet is not suitable if your pet has a skin problem.

One way to ensure the skin and coat stays shiny and soft is regular bathing. The frequency of baths is not as often as you think. It's not a weekly regime and certainly not daily. Surprising? Yes. But dogs don't need to take a bath as often as you want them to. It really depends on the kind of , the length and thickness of the coat. You want to keep essential oils from stripping off the skin and coat as best as you can.

It is good to use a moisturizing shampoo that will not irritate or cause a reaction on the skin when you bathe your pet. They also benefit from natural conditioners which contain essential vitamins such as Vitamin E.

Give them something fishy! Your cat isn't the only one that likes fish treats; your dog will love them too. They're delicious to them. So the next time you feed them, try adding some tuna, sardines or salmon to the dogs food. These three have omega-3 fatty acids that make healthy skin and coats.

If you are unsure about any alternative remedies being recommended, or wonder if they are good for your pet, ask your vet about it. Generally, most of the remedies with the proper dosage are great ways to make the skin and coat look healthier and shinier. One example people are using these days is **Spirulina**. It contains Vitamin B, carotenoids and protein.

Kelp is rich in essential nutrients, especially iodine which supports regular thyroid function, and helps to maintain optimum coat and skin conditions.

Kelp

Because there are many skin conditions and complaints, it is not always possible for a lay person to accurately diagnose the ailment. Even a professional health worker at times can only identify the problem by doing a simple skin scrape, or a biopsy in the most severe cases. Many skin conditions can be attributed to an allergic reaction, but unless the cause can be identified, it can be difficult to treat. One of the first things to check is that there are no parasites lurking on the skin. If not, the next most likely cause is dermatitis or eczema, or possibly a condition called pyoderma.

Eczema and Dermatitis

The Symptoms of eczema and dermatitis are inflamed hot skin, itchiness and redness. Normally this can be seen on the belly or under the armpits, any area where the coat is thinner. Sometimes hair loss is present where the animal has scratched the irritation severely. If hair loss has occurred because of scratching, you can give **Evening Primrose oil capsules or liquid**. It encourages re-growth and will aid and maintain the skin back to a normal balance.

Evening Primrose

Comfrey & Callendula Balm found in many alternative pet shops, is suitable to use externally on affected areas. It will soothe sore, dry or scaly and damaged skin during the treatment.

Callendula

Food intolerance

If your pet's condition is due to food intolerance, the most important thing is to try to eliminate what it is. To begin, try a bland diet consisting of mainly white meat and fish for a month. You can add boiled rice which is proven to be beneficial in increasing the rate of recovery. Later on you can add a good quality biscuit meal, but be aware that some dogs may be Gluten sensitive.

It is also advisable to avoid foods that contain colouring or flavouring agents, high protein foods and red meat meats. All of these have been known to cause allergic reactions in some Animals. If your pet is prone to skin problems, it is beneficial to try and keep him on a white meat diet.

They say you have to be cruel to be kind. How many times have we put food down and our pets have turned their noses up because it does not have the appetizing smell that some dog food contains? The smell is a trick to make our Animals eat more, but, in fact, they are so polluted with additives that they are actually harmful to our Animals. A lot of the time this manifests itself into a skin allergy or intolerance.

Unfortunately we now have the task of retraining our to eat healthy, just like us!

I discovered purely by chance a little health shop for dogs that specializes in organic food. The main component being that everything is grain-free, so if your pet has sensitive skin it could be coming from the inside of his system. I have been feeding organic food to my dogs for a couple of weeks now and, although the initial response was noses sniffing and then walking away, they are now actually enjoying it. I have seen a vast improvement in the scratching and irritation, so it is well worth investigating the ingredients in the dry food your pet has been eating.

If you find a good supplier of organic food, hopefully they will also specialize in **Botanical Herbs** for . A very good one, if your pet has itchy skin, is **chickweed drops**. It also has all around high nutritional benefits.

If you can find a cream or a paste called **Marigold petals**, it will calm and soothe infected or itchy skin when used as an ointment.

Marigold petals

Hot Spots

You wake up one morning and notice a small bald patch on your pet. At first it's the size of a pea and by lunchtime it has multiplied threefold.

They may have what we call a hot spot, so named because it is a circle of inflammation caused by your pet scratching, rubbing, licking or biting their way into the baldness. Vets normally call this pyotraumatic dermatitis, normally caused by a flea irritating the skin.

Clean the area well and, if possible, also try to trim around the reddened area. If it is too sore your pet will normally not allow you to do this. Apply a soft compress as this will ease any discomfort, and also soften any crusted areas that may have formed. Strong black or green tea dabbed on the area will help to dry the area and promote healing as the tea contains tannic acid. Do not apply this hot; it must be cool to the touch. Soothe the inflammation with Vitamin E cream. Another natural remedy is to use a leaf from an Aloe Vera plant. I have done this myself when I have had a burn so I know it has a nice, cool feeling when applied.

Hot Spots can also be caused by food allergies as previously discussed, so if fleas are not present, follow the same protocol for treating the skin, but also keep an eye on the diet.

Fleas and Ticks

If the irritation on the skin is caused by fleas, we don't have to treat with poisons. Many home remedies are already at hand in your kitchen. Adding a few drops of dishwashing detergent to your 's bath will kill any fleas. Be sure to thoroughly rinse to avoid any further skin irritations. If you see an invasion of fleas and the infestation is out of control, then obviously home remedies are not the solution, but hopefully we have not let it get that far.

Fleas apparently do not like brewer's yeast. Research has not confirmed this fact yet, but many pet owners and vets are convinced it works.

Add one to three teaspoons of brewer's yeast (depending on the dogs size) to your pet's food each day before the start of flea season and continue it throughout the season. You can also get a supplement containing brewer's yeast, garlic, zinc and biotin.

You can also use brewer's yeast topically by diluting one quarter cup with thirty-two ounces of water. Make sure it is dissolved by shaking well, and transfer to a spray bottle. You can then spray directly onto the fur and work it in well.

Another topical remedy is citrus peel. Research has shown that the component of D-Limonene present in the peel is deadly to all stages of cat flea, the same should apply to your dog .

Slice one or two lemons or limes with the peel still intact, and add to thirty-two ounces of hot water. Allow the mixture to soak for a few hours and after a cooling off period, use a spray bottle and rub the solution into the fur gently. If you want to be more adventurous you can use freshly squeezed orange juice and smear it through the coat, but this is quite sticky and I can't promise your dog will like or appreciate you doing this.

Many veterinarians like the idea of using garlic and they believe it works, although not much is written scientifically to prove this fact. Allicin and Alliin are present in garlic, which are a sulphur compound with medicinal properties. It's not as easy to get your animal to take it, but if you can chop a clove up and mix it in with some mince they might be fooled into taking it.

If you really want to see fleas jumping off your pet, try this next remedy!

Fleas do not like this and if you decide to use it, make sure you are outdoors.

Rose geranium oil

Rose Geranium

This oil is derived from the leaves of the Pelargonium graveolens plant, one of the scented geraniums. This particular oil has been known to repel ticks and fleas when applied to the skin of your dog . Some commercial products sold for repelling ticks actually contain rose geranium oil. The best way of using this is to put a few drops on your dogs collar. If you see evidence that a tick has made its home on your dog place a drop of geranium oil directly onto the tick and the nasty little critter should just drop off.

Lavender oil

Lavender

This product mixed with **sweet almond oil** will not rid your dog of fleas, but it will certainly repel them. Mix ten drops of lavender oil and five drops of almond oil in a spray bottle and shake well. Completely cover your , taking care to avoid the face and ears. I would suggest doing this outdoors, because if the little critters do decide to jump off, you don't really want them in your home.

Sweet Almond

Rosemary

This particular herb can repel fleas in a couple of ways.

Treat your pet's sleeping area by grinding fresh rosemary leaves into a powder and sprinkling on their bed.

Next, boil one half cup of leaves in a pint of water for thirty minutes and add the mixture to a gallon of warm water. Put your dog in a bath and completely soak the coat with this mixture, taking care to avoid the eyes and ears. Allow it to dry naturally. They will smell nice and the anti-inflammatory properties present in this herb will alleviate any itching.

Many home remedies used by pet owners are passed on to one another. Dog owners are like a small community when out walking and I have met many lifelong friends this way. I think the dogs are often attracted to each other first and then conversations start. One particular conversation started when I was in the woods walking my dog and for some reason unbeknown to me, my dog decided it would be nice to roll in Fox faeces. I warned the other dog owner not to approach as the smell was grotesque. He told me to go home and to smear tomato ketchup all over my pet's fur in the places he had rolled. The acid in the ketchup neutralized the smell and broke it down, until I was ready to spray him off without throwing up! The same thing is recommended by Americans whose animals are suddenly sprayed by a Skunk.

Vomiting

It is quite normal for your dog to occasionally decide he wants to throw up or vomit on your carpet. Like dogs, they get upset stomachs or, if they have been scavenging at the park or woods, they may have some food or plant material stuck in the throat. If this is the case, they normally self-medicate by finding the nearest clump of grass and chew enough that they either dislodge it or it will clear anything in the stomach making them feel poorly.

If it looks more serious because they are vomiting blood, this could be a sign of infection, worms or a liver or kidney disease. Go through the check list to see if your dog needs to see a vet.

- Is there any blood in the vomit?

- Does his stomach look distended or bloated?

- Very important, is he in pain?

- Is he trying to vomit but can't? (dry heaves)

- Are his gums pale or yellow?

- Does he also have diarrhoea?

- If they have any of the above signs or symptoms, please call your vet immediately.

The best course of action for an animal that is sick due to an upset stomach because of something they have eaten is fasting for twenty-four hours. This will allow the toxins to be removed from their systems. They may have become dehydrated so it is important that they have plenty of fluids. But only when the vomiting has subsided or it will just make them vomit all over again.

They should try to drink small amounts at first. I always have a syringe handy and I gently give just a few ounces at a time. Another option is to allow them to lick ice cubes if they cannot tolerate water. They will consume the water slowly and, because it is such a small amount, it will stay down better. You can also place some ice cubes in their water bowl.

Once they feel well enough to begin eating again, the first few meals should be bland and easy for them to digest like boiled white rice. If they keep the rice down, you can introduce small amounts of boiled white chicken. As vomiting robs the body of vital nutrients and minerals, it is good to add a multi-mineral supplement to their food for a few weeks.

It is also beneficial to buy a good probiotic supplement like acidophilus. There are many available for Animals as it is widely known to help the digestive tract by restoring good bacteria, especially if the vomiting has been prolonged and accompanied by a dose of diarrhoea.

Ginger is a popular natural treatment for nausea and vomiting in dogs, and has since gained support that the same can be said for dogs. Give one drop of ginger tincture per pound of body weight, normally twice a day in their water. You can also use **ginger tea** if the vomiting has stopped.

Ginger

Baking soda water can be given to try to stem the vomiting. Try the following recipe:

One teaspoon of baking soda

Half a cup of water

Try to give a few sips every few hours. If they are feeling poorly, you can use a plastic syringe gently placing a few ml into the side of the mouth.

Chamomile will calm and help with an upset stomach. Give two drops of tincture per pound of your dog's weight in water three times daily.

Chamomile

If you need to make your dog vomit because you believe they have swallowed something when foraging around in the garden or on a walk, the best solution is one teaspoon of hydrogen peroxide. It does not taste pleasant, but it will do the job and induce a foamy vomit. If this is successful and the object is clearly seen, then a follow up mixture should be given after a few hours.

One teaspoon of baking soda

One capsule of probiotic powder

Mix with half cup of warm water

Again, please give this with a plastic syringe. Once should do the trick.

Charcoal

In case of emergency if you know your dog has taken a toxic or poisoning substance and they have not vomited, the best thing to give is **charcoal** until you can visit the vet. This substance can hold many times its weight in toxic substances. The benefit is that it will absorb as quickly as possible whatever poison is in the system and be eliminated through the bowel. You can either open a capsule and put in a syringe or mix with some food and force feed with something nice like yoghurt or cheese. Administering this makes a difference in a time of crisis, but it is still imperative that you get to the vet as soon as possible.

Charcoal

Wound Care

Because our Animals are so mischievous they will get up to all sorts, either playing with other dogs or involved in a vicious dog fight. Hopefully it is not the latter as this can be serious and will need to be treated at once by a vet. However, if they have a superficial wound, infection bite or even a sting, there are home remedies that you can use and apply immediately.

Wounds, cuts and grazes

Most minor cuts and wounds can be dealt with quite easily at home. If you rushed your pet to the vet's office every time he got into a scrape, you would be forever there, which is not good for you or your pet.

A couple of homoeopathic remedies good for cleaning out any wound or cut are **calendula and hypericum.** They both come in tincture form and are easy to use. Calendula is from the marigold plant and is considered a vulnerary agent–a substance that promotes healing.

Hypericum facilitates wound healing and minimize pain.

A good essential oil and one of the best to use is **tea tree oil.** Taken from the paper bark tree of Australia, it was originally discovered by the aborigines. It is a powerful natural antiseptic that also has anti-bacterial properties. Unlike many other essential oils, tea tree is gentle enough to be applied directly to the skin.

Tea Tree oil

Aloe Vera applied externally on a wound is ideal for an animal. You can first use a mild Aloe Vera soap to cleanse and clean the wound or cut. Doing this first will eliminate any foreign bodies like dirt, grit or stones.

You can then apply an Aloe Vera gel which will heal the wound faster than any other conventional product. It has remarkable qualities which accelerate the process of cell renewal, preventing any infections from occurring.

Aloe Vera plant

Whilst I was working as a district nurse, I treated many patients with ulcerated legs. One of the treatments used at the time was **Manuka honey** and it is now being used extensively in the veterinary field.

Manuka flowers

147

Active manuka honey contains a unique compound "methylglyoxal" that provides a special natural antibacterial function able to block many infectious bacteria. The application of honey as a wound dressing reduces inflammation, clears infection, swelling and pain. It remains moist and seals the wound which will keep the bandage from sticking to the wound.

Manuka flowers

Try to prevent the dog from licking the honey off for at least twenty minutes to give the honey enough time to be absorbed by the skin. It is best to only use these treatments once a day for most wounds so as not to disturb the wound too much or to interrupt the healing process.

Bites and stings

One herb in particular is found in many gardens and has numerous antiseptic and healing benefits. It is called **Plantain.** If your dog has been in contact with poison ivy or oak, plantain can be used topically to help draw any toxins or splinters to the surface of the skin.

Plantains

Ideally, you should boil the plantain leaves in water and, using a washcloth, dip the mixture and apply over the area as a warm poultice. Use it several times daily for a few minutes until you see an improvement.

If the dog has been bitten or stung by an insect you will find the skin has been penetrated. This can cause redness, swelling and, in some cases, an infection. Make sure the area is clean and apply lavender oil. This is very soothing to the skin and will help ease any burning or stinging sensations.

Tea tree oils or geranium will help to ease the itching and relieve pain. We have recommended rescue remedy many times before as drops, but you can also use this as a cream and apply topically.

Geranium

For a wasp or bee sting, use **marigold ointment** to reduce the swelling, but not before you have removed the stinger with a pair of tweezers. Dab the area with some vinegar and then place a piece of fresh onion over it.

Aloe Vera in a gel or a spray will soothe and cool the affected area.

Bleeding

Do not be too alarmed if you see your dog has blood coming from a wound or cut. A small amount is nature's way of cleaning out any bacteria or dirt that may be present.

If your pet has a wound that is bleeding excessively, use a layer of wadding to bind the area and then apply a firm bandage. If the dog is only bleeding slightly from a minor cut or wound, sprinkle it with **cayenne pepper** from your kitchen pantry. Pepper enhances the clotting process and will stop the bleeding. Your may be experiencing shock so you can give either two drops of Bach flower rescue remedy directly on the tongue, or a homeopathic remedy called **Aconite 6c.**

Cayenne pepper

Because these medicines are absorbed through the mouth lining, they can be given to an unconscious dog. **Arnica** is the ideal medicine for cuts and bruises. Lavender oil helps to reduce inflammation and will encourage healing if the area is bruised.

Lavender

A good antiseptic rinse for wounds is a goldenseal tincture mixed with water. Another recommended remedy to stop bleeding is applying a cold compress of rosemary and witch hazel. To reduce bleeding and heal the wound, an Aloe Vera gel or spray can be applied directly to the affected area.

A dog has three pressure points which can be used to control the flow of blood if the bleeding is severe.

The upper inside of the front legs: This pressure point is used when you want to control any bleeding from the lower forelegs.

The upper inside of the rear legs: This pressure point is used when you need to control any bleeding from the lower hind legs.

153

The underside of the tail: This pressure point is used to control bleeding from the tail.

Please do not try to apply a tourniquet, instead try to put pressure on any of the above points by pressing gently until you can see a difference in blood loss. The next step is to trim hair around the wound. Doing this will help keep the wound clean and hopefully help the healing process. The danger from many wounds is not necessarily from bleeding, but from an infection that could set in later if the proper protocol is not followed.

If you do have to call the vet for a home visit, the best way to calm your pet is to keep him warm and comfortable and talk to them in a calm voice. Stroking the ears can be soothing to a distressed animal.

Once again, these measures are only if the wound or cut does not require urgent medical advice from a vet.

Many of the above recommendations in this book include products you already have in your home, but there are some you will have to purchase.

I am going to collate a first-aid package you can keep at home to use as needed.

It can be put together simply and inexpensively to start you off. Once you gain more knowledge, you can build a much larger stock of natural healing aids.

Basic First-Aid Kit For Dogs

1 **Tea tree**–this can either be used as an oil or a cream. It is highly effective in killing bacteria and germs because it possesses antiseptic and cleansing properties.

Use directly on burns or insect bites.

2. **Bach Flower remedies**.

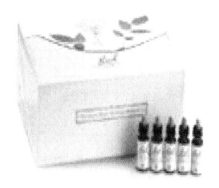

I recommend always having **rescue remedy** on hand as this is a first aid remedy for many emergencies, such as panic, loss of consciousness or shock. This calms and alleviates stress so your pet's mind and body quickly starts the healing process. There are various other flower remedies I have recommended for various situations. In time you can begin to add others.

3. **Lavender oil.** Lavender reduces inflammation and encourages healing and new growth while repairing scar tissue. Useful for treating cuts, abrasions, wounds and will soothe burns.

4. **Arnica**. Either tablets or cream are a good choice and should be used in case of shock or injury. It will help reduce swelling and heal bruised tissue. Tablet form can be given to calm the nerves after an injury. Please do not use arnica cream if the skin is broken.

5. **Witch Hazel** will stop bleeding, ease bruising and reduce inflammation if used externally. Good for cleaning a wound that is still bleeding.

6. **Aloe Vera** gel or spray is a great skin healer for cuts, burns and wounds. If you have an Aloe Vera plant at home, just break off one of the leaves and squeeze onto a burn for immediate relief.

It will also protect against infection and speed up the healing process.

7. **Activated charcoal** granules or capsules help to delay the absorption of toxins if your happens to have been poisoned. Also good for treating flatulence and digestive upsets.

8. **Comfrey**. This comes in ointment form and is especially good for healing broken bones and fractures. Apply once the bleeding has stopped on any wound as it is also an effective healer.

9. Keep some wadding and bandages handy in case you need to apply pressure to a wound to stop excessive bleeding until you can get them to the vet.

THE END

Anne Cambridge is lucky enough to live by the sea in Essex, and is able to take advantage of this fact and walk her two dogs on the beach. She has worked in the public sector for over 25 years as a trained nurse, but decided to take early retirement 9 years ago to concentrate and to fulfill her dreams of one day qualifying and becoming an alternative therapist.

She has achieved this ambition and is now successfully running her own Colonic Hydrotherapy clinic, and after completing her Diploma in Intolerance and Allergy testing is also able to offer clients this service.

As well as owning two Lhasa Apso dogs, Anne also has a cat called Felix and a budgie called Fred.

As well as **Dog Treatments & Alternative Home Remedies** Anne has also published

Gluten free diet made simple 100 Gluten free recipes for Breakfast, Dinner, Lunch, Deserts

Cat Treatments and Alternative Home Remedies

Made in the USA
Middletown, DE
06 December 2021